Heather Hammonds
Photographs by Lindsay Edwards

Contents

Goals

To make a clown **piñata** and play the **piñata game** at a party

Materials

To make the clown piñata, you will need:

- a balloon

- glue for the newspaper

- newspaper

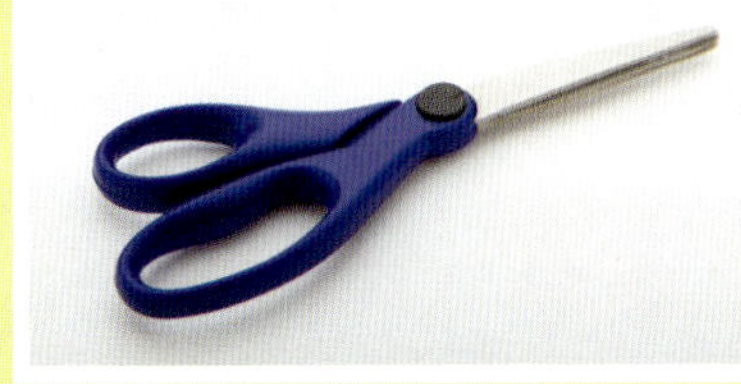

- scissors

- a bowl

- paints

- paintbrushes

- some string, 60 cm long

- lollies

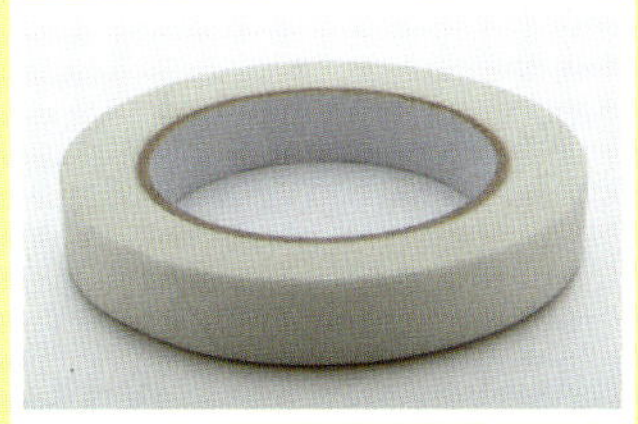

- tape

- yellow **streamers**

- glue for the streamers.

To play the piñata game, you will need:

- a **blindfold**

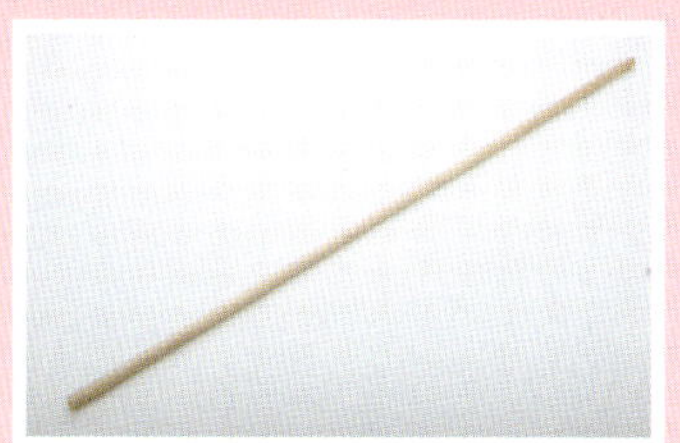

- a stick.

How to Make a Clown Piñata

1. Blow up the balloon and tie the end tightly so the air does not come out. An adult can help tie the balloon.

2. Cut the newspaper into lots of strips, about 10 cm long.

3. Put some glue into the bowl.

4. Put some newspaper strips into the glue.

5. Cover the balloon with the newspaper strips.
Do not cover the space near the end of the balloon.
You will need to put lollies into the end later.
Let the newspaper dry.

6. When the newspaper is dry,
glue some more strips onto the balloon.
Repeat this one more time.

7. Paint the newspaper with white paint and let it dry.
8. Paint a clown face onto the piñata.

9. Pop the balloon and carefully take it out of the piñata.
10. Ask an adult to help make two little holes in the top of the piñata with the scissors.

11. Push the string through the holes and tie it together. The string will make it easy to hang the piñata up later.

12. Pour the lollies into the piñata.

13. Cut some strips of tape and place them over the hole in the piñata, so the lollies do not fall out.

14. Paint the tape white and let it dry.

15. Cut the yellow streamers into lots of strips. Each strip needs to be 20 cm long.

16. Roll up two yellow strips, to make the clown's ears.

17. Glue an ear onto each side of the clown's head.

18. Glue the rest of the yellow strips onto the top of the clown's head, for its hair.

How to Play the Piñata Game

1. Hang the piñata up, before the party starts. Ask an adult to help you.
2. Put the piñata in a place where players can reach it with the stick.

3. Show the players where to line up. The line needs to be in a safe place, so no one gets hurt with the stick.

4. Tie the blindfold around the first player's eyes.

5. Take the player close to the piñata and give them the stick.

6. Then, stand well back from the player.

7. Ask the player to try to hit the piñata.
They must try to open it with the stick.

8. Give the player two turns.
If they do not open the piñata,
the next player has two turns.

9. Take the blindfold off the player when the piñata opens, and the lollies fall out.

Everyone can pick up the lollies and eat them!

Glossary

blindfold *(noun)*	a cloth that goes over the eyes, so a person cannot see
piñata *(noun)*	a decorated object filled with lollies
piñata game *(noun)*	a game where players hit a piñata, to open it and get lollies
streamers *(noun)*	long, thin strips of paper